GASLIGHTING: Stop Being Controlled

Harvey Norris, MSW, LCSW

TURTLE PRESS

ISBN-13: 978-1724988911
ISBN-10: 1724988913

FAIR USE ASSERTION

Any materials used in this book to illustrate and assist in comprehension, have been used under the Fair Use Copyright assertion of Section 107

Section 107 contains a list of the various purposes for which the reproduction of a particular work may be considered fair, such as criticism, comment, news reporting, teaching, scholarship, and research. Section 107 also sets out four factors to be considered in determining whether or not a particular use is fair:

- The purpose and character of the use, including whether such use is of commercial nature or is for nonprofit educational purposes
- The nature of the copyrighted work
- The amount and substantiality of the portion used in relation to the copyrighted work as a whole
- The effect of the use upon the potential market for, or value of, the copyrighted work

The distinction between fair use and infringement may be unclear and not easily defined. There is no specific number of words, lines, or notes that may safely be taken without permission. Acknowledging the source of the copyrighted material does not substitute for obtaining permission.

The 1961 Report of the Register of Copyrights on the General Revision of the U.S. Copyright Law cites examples of activities that courts have regarded as fair use: "quotation of excerpts in a review or criticism for purposes of illustration or comment; quotation of short passages in a scholarly or technical work, for illustration or clarification of the author's observations; use in a parody of some of the content of the work parodied; summary of an address or article, with brief quotations, in a news report; reproduction by a library of a portion of a work to replace part of a damaged copy; reproduction by a teacher or student of a small part of a work to illustrate a lesson; reproduction of a work in legislative or judicial proceedings or reports; incidental and fortuitous reproduction, in a newsreel or broadcast, of a work located in the scene of an event being reported. "Copyright protects the particular way authors have expressed themselves. It does not extend to any ideas, systems, or factual information conveyed in a work.

Table of Contents

What is Gaslighting?

It is the manipulation of one person by another with the intent to cause the manipulated person to doubt their own perceptions of the world around them and eventually their sanity. Their sanity is their belief in how well they are interpreting the events around them (*REALITY*). The feeling of *LOSS OF SANITY* is the fear that they are *UNABLE* to process events around them like other people, therefore they are no longer a part of society.

Origins of Gaslighting

In 1938 Patrick Hamilton wrote the British play "Angel Street" which came to America as a stage play called "Gas Light."

In 1944 it appeared in film as *Gaslight,* directed by George Cukor and starred Ingrid Bergman, Charles Boyer, Joseph Cotten, and 18-year-old Angela Lansbury in an Oscar-nominated screen debut.

The drama is about a woman whose husband slowly manipulates her into believing that she is going insane.

In the story, a husband attempts to convince his wife and others that she is insane by manipulating small elements of their environment and insisting that she is mistaken, remembering things incorrectly, or delusional when she points out these changes. The original title stems from the dimming of the gas lights in the house that happened when the husband was using the gas lights in the flat above while searching for the jewels belonging to a woman whom he had murdered.

The wife correctly notices the dimming lights and discusses it with her husband, but he insists that she merely imagined a change in the level of illumination.

The movie "Gas Light" is considered the first artistic portrayal of this type of psychological abuse.

Why is it harmful?

We are social animals and need to be part of the social group. Part of the whole. If you feel you cannot process events properly then you will begin to fear that the group will reject you and you will be alone.

It is important to remember that during ancient times the most extreme punishment was *EXILE* and not *DEATH*. Exile meant you had no one to watch after you, no one to support you and no one to care about and talk with.

Who can be a Gaslighter?

Anyone. There are no limitations. It does not require special training. Actually most of the learning experiences are *TRIAL & ERROR*. The Gaslighter tries something and if it works they learn to do it again. If it does not work, they try something else.

Who can be Gaslighted?

Anyone. Intelligence, age, level of education and dozens of other qualifications do not make a person immune from being *GASLIGHTED*.

What does it damage?

Our sense of our self. Our ability to feel safe and secure. Our ability to trust our interpretation of reality. The ability to interact with other human beings and the desire to help others and our willingness to allow them to help us. In short, it severs our ability to be part of the social group. A virtual death sentence.

How long does the damage last?

Until the person becomes aware of it and actively seeks to recognize it in all its forms. The only way to defeat Gaslighting is total awareness of it and its effects on your life. Without awareness, it can run from cradle to grave.

What is the power of words?

We interpret the world through symbols. Concepts. Ideas. The ocean is a concept. If you have never seen it, or a picture of it, it would be almost impossible to understand the vastness of it.

Words are our ways of putting a code to a construct. We use multiple words to describe a construct. A construct can have many forms but be the same construct. Confused? Not to worry. Just keep reading…

The construct we will be discussing is a solid object which can float on water and have things and people on top of it.

A BOAT.

If words had no power then we would only ever have to use the single word -- boat.

But a construct can have many forms. Therefore, many words to describe it.

How is a boat different from a yacht? From a barge? An ocean liner? A schooner? A houseboat? A bass boat? A rowboat? A pirate ship? A ferry? A steamboat? A paddle wheeler? A sailboat? A Ketch? An oil tanker?

The list can go on for quite a while. Each word brings a different picture to mind. Each word describes a single construct, but it also describes a specific type of construct with very specific differences.

How does our language change our thoughts?

The words we use to describe a construct alter our perception of the construct. If you were told your partner bought a sailboat, you might think of a 12-foot, single man Sunfish, or a 32-foot sailboat with a wheelhouse and sleeping quarters. The words I use to describe a construct cause different pictures to be created in your brain. Take a moment to note the use of the word brain instead of mind. *MIND & BRAIN* are two very different things. Philosophers have been arguing over them and the differences for centuries. Your *BRAIN* is an organ housed within your skull, made up of more than ten-billion nerve cells organized into many different smaller sections. Words create precise constructs in the brain. Your *MIND* is a philosophical construct which makes up your personality and sense of self. Use your words carefully.

Up to now we have been talking about objects. Let's expand ourselves to talk about actions.

The following three sentences convey the same action construct:

Sentence A: John hit the other man.
Sentence B: John punched the other man.
Sentence C: John knocked out the other man.

The Construct: a person named John came in physical contact with another person.

Each sentence has a different "feeling" to it.

Sentence A tells you John made physical contact with the other person. This contact may be accidental or intentional. It may have been severe or rather minor.

Sentence B tells you John made deliberate contact with the other person, specifically with his fist, and you may think John made the contact with a *SPECIFIC INTENT*.

Sentence C tells you John made physical contact with the other person and the resulting contact caused the person to lose consciousness.

The average person would grade these sentences as ranging from a minor issue in Sentence A to a very serious issue in Sentence C. And they would be interpreting it normally.

By the way, the word NORMAL indicates that multiple people would see the same event and all would retell the event in a very similar fashion.

When we change the words, we alter the construct and then alter how other people perceive the construct.

Why use the word perceive? Why did I not say _see the construct_ or _hear the construct_?

I once heard the Oxford-English Dictionary has about half-a-million words. In daily life we generally use between eight thousand and twelve thousand words. There are many words no one uses on a regular basis and some we probably have not used in fifty years but people are afraid to remove them.

Take the word *FLAPPER*. A Flapper was a young woman in the 1920's who went out to speakeasies drinking and smoking. Not a word you hear every day. Probably not a word you have used in the last decade, but it is still there, waiting to be revived.

Our senses are *PASSIVE, not ACTIVE*!
When our senses are triggered we call it a *SENSATION*. Sensations are created in us when external stimuli come to us, we do not go to them.

What is the differences between passive and active?

Passive is something which happens to us. When talking about our senses, it is information that bounces off of us. Active is something we do to something or someone else. This is a very important difference if we are to understand how we relate to the world. This is the first step toward awareness which allows us to protect ourselves from Gaslighting.

Why is our language active?

We are very active beings. We move around. We jump, talk, run, swing, hop, skip, have sex. We are constantly on the move. Who has not watched a three year old child, just mastering their legs, run back and forth for no other reason than they can. We are active. We create our understanding of the world. We use words to describe the world. We are active, therefore our language is active. It is also not accurate. Bear with me for a minute and read on about 'passive'. Then we will tackle the *ACTIVE-PASSIVE* Problem.

Why are our senses passive?

Our senses are passive because they stay inside our bodies. They do not reach out into the world. Your eyes do not leave your head and travel three miles away to be able to see a distant object, nor so do they travel to the full moon to explore the dark and light patterns on its surface.

They wait patiently in their sockets for light rays to bounce of the moon and eventually be absorbed by the eye, then cause nerves in the rear of the eye to activate (we call this activation 'firing') which then sends impulses to an area of the brain which then interprets them based on other things we have seen and our current emotional state.

All of this happens at a speed so fast, it is almost unthinkable.

Movement of an object causes a disturbance in the air which sends waves of air bouncing around. Eventually these waves of air bounce around and bounce off of our eardrum, which then causes attached nerves to fire, sending a signal to the part of our brain which interprets these things and we then perceive a *SOUND*. When the sound is part of a set of sounds we use to communicate, a language, and then even more processing occurs in different areas of the brain.

What is perception?

This is a complex question. In the end, perception is the final construct we create from the various activity in the world around us, received from our senses, mixed with our prior experiences, our biases and our desires. This is why many people can experience the same event and come away with very different memories of what happened.

> Outside information received by our senses
>   + Prior Experiences
>   + Our Biases
>   + <u>Our Desires</u>
>   = **Perception**

What is authenticity?

A state of mind that allows us to be aware of our prior experiences, biases and desires so we can allow our perception to be more accurate and in tune with outside reality.

> Outside information received by our senses
>   - Prior Experiences
>   - Our Biases
>   - <u>Our Desires</u>
>   = **Perception**

How do we achieve authenticity?

Another difficult question. With a deceptively simple answer. Say what you mean and hear what is being said. The problem is we have become so used to translating everything it is almost impossible to achieve this. To learn this skill becomes a process of learning yourself, which is a lifelong journey. Each month you will become better, and each year you will improve, but you will never master the process.

Step 1: Question everything you feel and hear to see if you are receiving the message that was presented.

Step 2: Practice STEP 1 every day.

Step 3: That is for a later time…

How does all this work with Gaslighting?

The Gaslighting is counting on you to use your prior experiences, biases, & desires to warp the information in a manner which allows them to control you.

A personal example:

When I was a child and would do something my mother did not like, she would tell my father. The following conversation would occur.

DAD: "When I get home we needed to talk."
ME: "What do we need to talk about?"
DAD: "We will talk about it later."
ME: "Can you tell me what it is?"
DAD: "We will talk later."

This is a classic control technique. It allowed my father to control the timing of the information release. It left me having to review everything I had done that might cause my father a problem. A chance to whip myself before my father introduced his self-esteem crushing agenda.

Let's revisit Gaslighting...

The Primary purpose of gaslighting it to control the other person by causing them to doubt the reality they are presented.

The Gaslighter's toolbox includes:
- rewriting history,
- denying reality,
- blame you for reacting to their abuse
- Refusing to take responsibility for their abuse

Gaslighting is a form of emotional abuse.

It is insidious. It sneaks into your mind and psyche. It begins it damage you before you are even aware of it.

When not addressed, gaslighting destroys self-esteem, fuels self-doubt, and cranks up anxiety,

Back to "What is Gaslighting?"

- It's when someone tells you that your interpretation of reality isn't true.

- They do harmful things and then deny ever doing those things.
- The do harmful things and minimize the details of it.
- They discount memories, evidence, and facts — in favor of lies.
- They often accuse you of doing things that they themselves are doing.
- They constantly rewrite history whenever convenient.
- This is "crazy-making."
- It is literally designed to makes the recipient feel crazy and question their own reality.

So, why do people gaslight?

To simply control.

Control almost always is fueled by fear.

Fear is sometimes known to the Gaslighter and sometimes not.

To the Gaslighter, everything they say is gospel and everything you say is wrong. They interrupt, make degrading comments, they dismiss facts & make it the victim feel stupid.

Is the person who is being Gaslighted really a victim?

Absolutely! It is important to accept yourself as being the victim so the process of change can begin. Once you understand you are being or have been victimized, you can begin rebuilding your life.

How common is gaslighting?

It is more common than most people think. Gaslighting is connected to two of the personality disorders. These are the narcissistic personality disorder and the borderline personality disorder. Both of these sets of traits have a very specific set of behaviors which present as poor boundaries.

- Boundaries are lines we draw in our own sandbox. Who am I? What do I stand for? What would I live for? What would I die for?

These boundaries are formed from beliefs which are learned very early in life.

Neither of these sets of traits or behaviors allow for accurate perception of the reality happening around the personality disordered person.

In general, narcissistic traits tend to lead to engaging in Gaslighting, and borderline traits tend to lead to being Gaslighted.

What Behaviors does the Gaslighter use?

- Withholding information from victim;
- Countering information to fit the abuser's perspective;
- Discounting information;
- Verbal abuse, usually in the form of jokes;
- Responding to everything with sarcasm;
- Blocking and diverting the victim's attention from outside sources;
- Trivializing the victim's worth;
- Undermining victim by gradually weakening them and their thought process.

Let's quickly walk through these behaviors in the real world. This is not an exhaustive description, but rather little bites of ideas. You are very capable of finding your own examples!

What Behaviors does the Gaslighter use?

—REVISITED—

Withholding information from victim;

The example I gave earlier about my father fits here. Also statements like:

- You don't need to know that.
- That's on a need to know basis.
- You wouldn't understand.
- You're too dumb to understand.

Countering information to fit the abuser's perspective;

- I know I yelled at you, but it was for your own good.
- I only hit you because you make me.
- You make me ...

Discounting information;

- Everyone knows that's wrong.
- You don't know what you are talking about.
- That's dumb.
- Only you could be that stupid.
- Right! (With sarcasm)

Verbal abuse, usually in the form of jokes;

- Like anyone would think that!
- Stupid people are allowed to like too.
- Do you know what is dumber than that...nothing!

Responding to everything with sarcasm;

- Really!
- Oh yeah!
- Riiiiiight!
- You didn't have to pay for that idea, did you?
- For thoughts like that, you need to go get your money back

Blocking and diverting the victim's attention from outside sources;

- *All TV news is wrong. (Fake)*
- *Those talking heads don't have a clue.*
- *Stop listening to those people.*
- *Don't watch anymore of that*

Trivializing the victim's worth;

- I am the only person who cares about you.

- Why would anyone want to be with a slob like you?
- No one will help you live I will.
- If you can find someone to put up with your stupid, go for it.
- You really are slow!

Undermining victim by gradually weakening them and their thought process.

- Don't worry about that!
- It's not your business.
- How could you think like that?
- Only idiots think that way!

Three Gaslighting Attacks

How do you know when you are being Gaslighted?

- You are repeatedly provoked and when you react you are blamed for overreacting or being too sensitive.
- When you confront the Gaslighter with their behavior and make them take responsibility they attack you and lash out, with the intent of blaming you!
- No matter what happens they are always the victim. No matter how provoking, disgusting or vile their behavior, they are misunderstood and attacked.
- The constant attacks cause you to start questioning your perception of the world around you. You start to disbelieve your emotions, your values and eventually you question who you are.

Let's take each one separately.

The Provoking Attack: The Gaslighter wants two things. To control you and to focus all scrutiny away from themselves. They do not want to be assessed, screened, or put under the microscope. They achieve this by picking at you and provoking you. They learn the things that provoke you, often called "chinks in your armor" and they stab you.

—- when someone says "they are pushing my buttons…" they are describing this experience.

Step 1:

They provoke you until you become angry and aggressive, then they tell you your response is out of proportion to the provocation. They attack. They make statements like...

- You are overreacting!
- You are hysterical!
- You are crazy!
- You are too sensitive!
- You are negative!
- You are paranoid!
- You are bipolar!

- You are mentally ill!

Step 2:

Adding insult to injury they tell you to "calm down" or "relax".

The goal of this step is to make you feel embarrassed by your reaction. To make you feel ashamed. To make you doubt yourself.

Step 3:

They tell everyone how unstable you are.

The goal is to put you down while getting "pats on the back" about how benevolent they are. How caring. How willing you are to sacrifice for them.

Step 4:

Rinse and repeat.

Analysis: Why this works!

Remember the Dr. Seuss story 'The Cat in the Hat'? Thing One is not very bad. Thing Two is also not bad when alone. Neither is Thing Three. But when Thing One is followed by Two who is followed by Three, followed by Four, then Five, Six, and Seven, you lose it.

You have been overwhelmed. Hit by a tidal wave. When you react, they point out that you reacted to Thing Seven, and Seven was minor. They deny the existence of Things One through Six. If you buy this, it certainly seems that you are overreacting.

The Mirror Attack: In this dance the first move is made by the victim, the response is made by the Gaslighter.

Step 1:

You get tired of being provoked so you muster all your rational thoughts and calmly point out the Gaslighter's misbehavior.

Step 2:

The Gaslighter attacks.

- They become verbally abusive!
- They will twist your words!
- They will throw arguments back in your face.
- They will deny reality.
- They will use the "What about…" technique.

If these fail,

- They escalate the attack by hurling completely outrageous accusations at you, trying to destabilize you.
- They put you on the defense.

Step 3:

- You find yourself on the defensive.
- Your attempt collapses
- You may even identify so deeply with the Gaslighter that you begin to apologize.

Analysis: Why do they do this?

Gas-lighters have a very poorly developed 'sense of self'. Their Ego is very fragile. An attack on their behavior is a direct attack on their identity.

A person with a fragile Ego does not see themselves as separate from their actions.

A person with a strong Ego can say, "I am a good person who has acted in a bad, or selfish manner".

The fragile Ego says, "I am a bad person." Or "I am a good person."

When the Mirror Attack starts, they perceive you as trying to destroy who they are, their very identity. They will fight to the death.

Before we continue...

<u>The "What About" technique.</u>

This is a way of arguing as an attempt to misdirect the fight.

You: "You are being mean and nasty!"

GSL: "What about John, he is ALWAYS mean and nasty!"

You: "Yes he is, but we are talking about you and not John."

GSL: "Why not talk about John, he is always mean and nasty! Why, just last week…"

(Clinical Social Workers & Mental Health Counselors often have problems responding to this technique. You're not alone.)

Playing the Victim Card: In this dance, the Gaslighter is always the victim.

Step 1:

The Gaslighter starts by playing the "oh poor me" role or the more extreme "poor pitiful me" role.

Step 2:

- They abuse, criticize, judge, lie, and betray others, threaten, and smear other people because they are the victim.
- By the power of their victimhood, all of their nasty and brutish behavior is in reality, benevolent behavior, because they are the true victim.
- They are the true downtrodden!
- They accuse you of pretending to be the victim as a way of attacking you!

Step 3:

You are the Bad One.

- No matter how you respond, the Gaslighter will still run around telling everyone you are the lunatic.
- They will tell everyone you are obsessed with them.

Analysis: What can you do?

Very little!

This Gaslighter is so busy misdirecting and attacking, they have no time for loyalty or integrity.

Patience, kindness, openness, empathy and compassion are useless in this situation.

To the Gaslighter, these responses are for suckers, or weaklings, who deserve whatever happens to them.

Buying the Abuse

The Self-Abuse Cycle

When you are constantly questioning your emotions, the interpretation of events around you, your sense of worth, and your very identity, you begin to distrust yourself. Thoughts come into your head unbidden, like:

- That can't be right!
- I must have misunderstood!
- He did not really mean what he said!
- He just says that because I make him angry!
- She must know I did not mean to question her authority!
- Why do I always do this dumb stuff!
- He's right, nobody would want me!

- I am lucky she puts up with me!

Now comes the long term damage to your sense of self.

- You stop trusting yourself.
- You doubt others.
- Every decision causes anxiety.
- Every interaction leads to a feeling if depression as you wonder, "did I get it right?"
- The constant second-guessing leads to exhaustion.
- You stop trusting yourself!
- You over analyze every interaction!
- You ruminate on every small detail!
- You feel disconnected from your sensations and body as well as your emotions.

Where do we find Gaslighting in our daily lives?

Well, everywhere. Combating gaslighting requires self-awareness and critical thinking skills.

Gaslighting occurs in our personal and professional relationships, our schools, lunchrooms, job sites, and doctor's office. It also exists in the media. More on that in a little bit.

Most gaslighting is caused by sloppy thinking, bad judgement and misinformation. Most of it is not intended.

About 3% of the population shows the character traits of the narcissistic personality disorder and the borderline personality disorder. These are called the DRAMATIC personality disorders.

People with these personality traits often use gaslighting as a function of getting their needs met. Sometimes it is premeditated, like a con job, other times it is simply using a skill they have used so often, they do not realize they are actually using it.

When is gaslighting intentional?

When it is used deliberately to manipulate and coerce people. People with the dramatic PD traits use gaslighting in everyday communication.

Media outlets involved in pushing a very specific point of view also use gaslighting to twist facts and ideas to twist information. As a general rule, when a media site or television station identifies itself as an outlet for a specific type of partisan idea, they are advertising their gaslighting.

For example, the following statements identify the use of gaslighting:

Station KABC: The Voice of the Conservative.

Station WXYZ: A Progressive Voice in your Community

Life Threatening Gaslighting.

There is one group of individuals who deliberately use gaslighting. They may not even know what to call it, but the techniques are unmistakable.

These are the Predator Gaslighters. We will look at them in three different groups.

- Domestic Violence Perpetrators
- Sexual Abusers
- Abusive Parents

Domestic Violence Perpetrators and gaslighting.

Predatory Gaslighters like the Domestic Violence Perpetrator (DVP) use gaslighting to control the life of their partner and eventually to destroy and crush their individuality until they are permanently and emotionally enslaved. Those victims which try to escape are, 9 out of 10 times, murdered by their partners.

Why is the murder rate so high?

When a person who creates their identity, on the idea that they can permanently and totally control another person, and that control fails the DVP's identity collapses.

They no longer have an anchor in their life and lose their sense of self.

When a DVP says, "I can't live without you!"

What they are actually saying is if my ability to control you fails, I have to look at the REAL ME.

The DVP's REAL ME is horrifying to them. They would rather die than face themselves.

Often they project this anger outward, kill the partner and then, when they realize there is no escape for their actions they kill themselves.

Are you being gaslighted by a predator in your relationship? The following tactics are regularly used by DVP's to control their victim. Ask yourself the following questions. Has or does your partner ever….

- Insult, demean or embarrass you with put-downs?
- Control what you do, who you talk to or where you go?
- Look at you or act in ways that scare you?
- Push you, slap you, choke you or hit you?
- Stop you from seeing your friends or family members?
- Control the money in the relationship?
- Take your money or Social Security check, make you ask for money or refuse to give you money?
- Make all of the decisions without your input or consideration of your needs?
- Tell you that you're a bad parent or threaten to take away your children?

- Prevent you from working or attending school?
- Act like the abuse is no big deal, deny the abuse or tell you it's your own fault?
- Destroy your property or threaten to kill your pets?
- Intimidate you with guns, knives or other weapons?
- Attempt to force you to drop criminal charges?
- Threaten to commit suicide, or threaten to kill you?

If these are happening to you, seek outside help. Statistics show 9 out of 10 people who leave these relationships, are at risk of severe violence and death.

Sexual Abusers and Gaslighting.

The Sexual Abuse Predator (SAP) is one of the most damaging and violent predators and the damage they cause often has a life-long effect on the victim. Once again they are using gaslighting for control.

Examples of Sexual Child Abuse include:

- Fondling a child's genitals.
- Having intercourse with a child.
- Having oral sex with a child.
- Having sex in front of a child.
- Having a child touch an older person's genitals.
- Using a child in pornography.
- Showing X-rated books or movies to a child.

When committing their crimes they manipulate and force children with statements designed to damage their perception of reality.

Examples of the SAP's gaslighting include:
- "If you tell your mother/father, I will call you a liar and they will believe me."
- "If you tell anyone I will kill your mother/father."
- "If your mother/father find out, they will think you are a slut/whore and will hate you."
- "You know you want me to do this."

- "If you let me do this, I will not do this to your sister/brother and you can keep them safe."

Abusive Parents and Gaslighting.

Some Abusive Parents (ABP) intend to hurt their children, but most do not. ABP's hurt children because they lack the skills to properly parent, control their aggression, and de-escalate themselves to avoid hurting their children.

Some reasons an ABP may hurt their children include:
- Lose their tempers when they think about their own problems.
- Don't know how to discipline a child.
- Expect behavior that is unrealistic for a child's age or ability.
- Have been abused by a parent or a partner.
- Have financial problems.
- Lose control when they use alcohol or other drugs.

Physical Child Abuse - an example:

Michelle picked up her 19-month old child, Jaquan, from daycare after a 12-hour work shift. She changed Jaquan's diaper at daycare, and when she arrived home 30 minutes late he had pooped again. She got angry. She was tired. Instead of changing his diaper, she decided to give him a bath. She filled the sink with water, took off his diaper and put him in the sink. Jaquan immediately started screaming. Michelle had enough. She started slapping Jaquan and telling him to shut up. When he would not stop crying she lifted him from the sink and noticed scald marks and burns on his small body. The water was too hot.

When she took him to the emergency room she was interviewed by child protective services. She made the following statements:
- "It was a long day and I have had no help for months."
- He is always cranking and ever sleeps through the night so I am always tired."

- If he had not been screaming, I would not have slapped him."

All of these statements are examples of an attempt to gaslight the interviewer. Each statement blames the child or someone else. Each statement transfers control of the ABP's actions to someone else.

Classic gaslighting includes a refusal to accept responsibility for your actions.

Examples of Physical Child Abuse
- Shaking or shoving.
- Slapping or hitting.
- Beating with a belt, shoe or other object.
- Burning a child with matches or cigarettes.
- Scalding a child with water that is too hot.
- Pulling a child's hair out.
- Breaking a child's arm, leg, or other bones.
- Not letting a child eat, drink or use the bathroom.

It takes a lot to care for a child. A child needs food, clothing and shelter as well as love and attention. Parents generally want to provide these things, but have other pressures and lack of skills as well.

Refusal to accept responsibility for your actions is a form of gaslighting.

Critical Thinking Skills

What is critical thinking?

The ability to think clearly and rationally. The ability to understand the logical connection between ideas. The ability to engage in independent thinking. The ability to be reflective about information you learn.

Rational thinking is based on logic, instead of impulse or whimsy. It means the ability to reason.

Logical thinking is a process of clearly moving from one related thought to another.

Independent thinking is the use of rational and logical thought when taking in or reviewing information.

Reflective thinking is the consequence of independent thinking.

How to Develop Critical Thinking!

Try to be aware of everything around you.

We need to use basic observing. Increase our observation skills. Start small!

> **Observation Exercise:** When you walk into a room try to observe what color shoes people are wearing. Do this without being caught. Next day, try it with shirts, or ties, etc. Add something to your list every couple of days. Then start doing this exercise at different times of the day and in different places. You will be amazed at how fast your observational skills increase.

Analyze what you see.

Joan is wearing red high heels and Cindy is wearing flats, while Matthew is wearing black shoes with white athletic socks.

Interpret what you see using evaluation and inference.

Cindy was complaining about her ankles hurting several weeks ago so maybe that is why she is wearing flats. Joan is wearing a new red dress and her boyfriend is coming back into town after a long business trip, so maybe she is looking forward to a romantic evening. Matthew normally dresses well but has been quieter than usual. Eventually you observe he is not wearing his wedding band. Do the white socks with black shoes have anything to do with marital discord and possible couch surfing?

Reflect on your observations.

Think about other things you have noticed in the past and imagine how they might be attributable to what you are observing today.

Joan had been talking more about the success of her boyfriend in his new job and Matthew used to sit around on break and listen to the 'girl talk' but now stays at his desk and makes excuses about being overworked.

Now you have reached a possible explanation about Joan and Matthew's behavior.

Problem Solving and Decision Making.

Now you have an idea about the events in Joan and Matthew's life, you can decide if you want to help either one of just continue to observe. By your observations, you have increased your internal control and therefore your personal power.

Using Critical Thinking to Evaluate Arguments, Advertising or Propaganda.

We have all been driving down the road and seen the Billboard sign that says:

Does Advertising Work?

It Just Did!

You Looked!

Proof positive. You looked. It works. We should all go rent a roadside billboard.

Or should we?

Advertising is the presentation of information. Did this sign present information? YES!

The purpose of advertising is to present information with the intent of making you want to buy or change something.

Just noticing it is relatively worthless.

If it did not change your behavior then the advertising failed. Money spent without return.

At the end of this manuscript, I will analyze a movie blurb I read today to help better understand this concept.

Different Ways to Think Critically

The Basic Method

Some person or some media outlet has told you something recently and you want to review it in a critical thinking manner.

The Basic Method has you ask yourself six simple questions about information you have just heard. Here they are…

Question 1: Who said it?

- Someone you know?
- Someone in a position of authority or power?
- Does it matter who told you this?

Question 2: What did they say?

- Did they give facts or opinions?
- Did they provide all the facts?
- Did they leave anything out?

Question 3: Where did they say it?

- Was it in public or in private?
- Did other people have a chance to respond and provide an alternative account?

Question 4: When did they say it?

- Was it before, during or after an important event?
- Is timing important?

Question 5: Why did they say it?

- Did they explain the reasoning behind their opinion?
- Were they trying to make someone look good or bad?

Question 6: How did they say it?

- Were they happy or sad, angry or indifferent?
- Did they write it or say it?
- Could you understand what was said?

The Critical Consensus Method

This method comes from a scientific paper presented by B. K. Scheffer and M.G. Rubenfeld in the Journal of Nursing Education. Scheffer and Rubenfeld present critical thinking skills as seven separate functions.

Each function is an *ACTIVITY*.

Activity 1: Analyzing

Separating or breaking a whole into parts to discover their nature, functional and relationships.

"I studied it piece by piece"
"I sorted things out

Activity 2: Applying Standards

Judging according to established personal, professional, or social rules or criteria.

"I judged it according to..."

Activity 3: Discriminating

Recognizing differences and similarities among things or situations and distinguishing carefully as to category or rank.

"I rank ordered the various..."
"I grouped things together"

Activity 4: Information Seeking

Searching for evidence, facts, or knowledge by identifying relevant sources and gathering objective, subjective, historical, and current data from those sources.

"I knew I needed to lookup/study..."
"I kept searching for data."

Activity 5: Logical Reasoning

Drawing inferences or conclusions that are supported in or justified by evidence.

"I deduced from the information that..."
"My rationale for the conclusion was..."

Activity 6: Predicting

Envisioning a plan and its consequences.

"I envisioned the outcome would be..."
"I was prepared for..."

Activity 7: Transforming Knowledge

Changing or converting the condition, nature, form, or function of concepts among contexts.
"I improved on the basics by..."
"I wondered if that would fit the situation of ..."

Courtesy of B. K. Scheffer and M.G. Rubenfeld, "A Consensus Statement on Critical Thinking in Nursing," Journal of Nursing Education, 39, 352-9 (2000).

Which method you use is completely up to you. These are not the only two methods. You can also create your own method. The reward comes from going through the process, not using steps or activities blindly.

Critical Thinking in Action:

Remember:

The main intention of the Gaslighter is to target the victim's mental equilibrium, self-confidence and self-esteem. It is a dangerous form of abuse because it undermines the mental stability of the victim, who becomes depressed and withdrawn and totally dependent on the abuser for their sense of reality.

To fight back you need to be able to:

- Think about a topic or issue in an objective and critical way.
- Identify the different arguments there are in relation to a particular issue.
- Evaluate a point of view to determine how strong or valid it is.
- Recognize any weaknesses or negative points in the argument.

- Notice what implications there might be behind a statement or argument.
- Provide structured reasoning and support for an argument that we wish to make.

Zani: the example:

Zani is an African-American female who Works as a stocker in a local dollar store. She's held the job for approximately three years. Her father is Mexican and her mother is a African-American. Her youngest child's father was African-American.

Her current boyfriend is white and is very controlling. He insists on dropping her at the store and picking her up. He refuses to allow her to take the bus home. He often calls to check on her several times a day. He has been overheard telling her that she's not smart enough to get home on her own and she needs him.

She recently confided in a friend that he checks her phone every night and looks at all of her text messages. When her friend asked her how she feels about her boyfriend, she states that her baby's father used to physically beat her and threatened to kill her, but her new boyfriend keeps her safe.

When she asked her white male manager to move from stocking to working or cash register, he told her that he did not think she was smart enough to do it, because "anyone who can't figure out what type of man they should be dating, certainly is not capable of handling money."

She recently borrowed money from her coworker in order to buy a pack of cigarettes, because her boyfriend refused to give her the money. Her friend asked her what she did with the money she earned and she stated her boyfriend takes it every pay day and only gives her what he thinks she needs. She said that was OK because she doesn't feel she would handle the money properly anyway.

Is Zani the victim of gaslighting?

She has been told by the store manager and by her boyfriend that she is unable to handle money.

Is there any evidence that supports this?

Her manager stated he did not believe she could handle money because of her choice of boyfriends.

Is this a racial comment?

Was the manager trying to be racial and discriminatory?

Has anyone ever seen her handle money inappropriately?

Her boyfriend told her that he has to drop her off and pick her up because she's not smart enough to be able to take the bus home or find another way home.

Is there any proof that she can't take a bus home?

Are there any other reasons boyfriend might drop her off and pick her up?

Is it possible this is a method for the boyfriend to control her, and know where she is at all times?

What could possibly be the reason for her boyfriend to check her cell phone and review all of her texts and calls every night?

Is this behavior meant to protect her, as the boyfriend seems to say it is?

Why does the boyfriend call multiple times during the day to check on her?

Is he afraid she's going to get lost in the store?

Why does the boyfriend take her paycheck every week and only give her the money he wants her to have?

Is there any reason, from the information given, that she needs this kind of financial oversight?

When you start asking questions like this, you begin to see patterns of behavior that may not make any sense. At first glance you might overlook certain things, if you did not ask questions.

The most likely explanation for the boyfriend dropping her off and picking her up, not letting her take the bus home, taking her paychecks and giving her back only the money he wants., checking her cell phone every day for calls and text, is that she is in a domestically violent relationship.

Domestic Violence does not have to have overt physical violence. All of these behaviors are behaviors that are seen in the Predatory Gaslighter known as the Domestic Violence Perpetrator. These behaviors by her boyfriend are designed to make her believe that she is incompetent, unable to do basic things, and needs him in order to keep her safe. All of these things chip away at her self-esteem and sense of identity. This is classic gaslighting.

Let's take a look at the manager. While his statements could certainly be interpreted as racist, they clearly undermine her feelings of self-worth and identity as an independent person.

They are also form of gaslighting. They are more petty and impersonal, and not directly predatory.

Is there any structured argument you could have or make that with support denying her access to her own money, her own transportation, and then on monitored phone?

Are there any weaknesses or negative points to the arguments that she should not have access to her money, more be allowed to attempt to be a cashier?

Given the information you have, is there any structured argument you could make to continue to Maine her access to what most of us consider to be basic human rights.

Everyone has the basic human right to control and handle their money.

Everyone has the basic human right to come and go as they please and not forced to hear to someone else schedule.

Everyone has the basic right to privacy in their communications.

In order to determine if gaslighting is occurring, you can also go back and ask yourself if you would allow someone to apply these behaviors to you.

How would you feel if your spouse or significant other demanded to go through your cell phone every night?

How would you feel if your spouse or significant other took your entire paycheck on payday and then only gave you back the money they thought you needed or deserved?

How would you feel if your significant other or spouse refused to allow you to ride the bus home and instead dropped you off and pick you up at work every day?

If any of these things happen to you, it is a good bet that gaslighting is occurring.

Politicians Use Gaslighting to Rewrite Reality.

President William Jefferson Clinton had a sexual contact with the female intern in the White House during his presidency. This lead to impeachment hearings. After initial denial that anything occurred, he settled on the statement "I did not have sex with that woman."

Was this gaslighting?

Remember, gaslighting is used to control and alter reality. The entire purpose is to make the people observing feel they have not seen what they have seen.

So let's review this.

Our society does not have a very clear definition of sex. When asked to define it, most people would have difficulty capturing the entire concept under one definition.

In general there are three specific aspects to heterosexual sex. These are vaginal intercourse, oral intercourse and anal intercourse. In this particular situation, the statement made by President Clinton inferred that the only real type of sex is vaginal intercourse.

Therefore, the oral sex he engaged in with the intern was not real sex, so it was not sex.

Culturally speaking, most Americans would define any type of genital contact to be sex. Therefore, the statements made by President Clinton were clearly gaslighting.

The attempted to alter the cultural reality of the definition of sex, and they attempted to sway the American people into thinking that sex did not occur.

President Clinton is far from being the only politician who is used gaslighting.

One of the Republican congressman who was involved in prosecuting President Clinton during the impeachment hearings had a secret. During the impeachment hearings the secret came out.

At the time of the hearing the congressman was in his mid-60s. It turned out the congressman had been involved in an adulterous affair in his mid-50s. While he admitted to the affair He described it as a youthful indiscretion. Since the affair not accidental it could not be called and indiscretion. Since the congressman was in his mid-50s when it occurred, and he had been married, at the time of the affair for decades, it could not be called youthful.

Most of the press conferences during the presidency of George W. Bush could be described as gaslighting extravaganzas.

The entire issue with President Barrack Obama being accused of being a Muslim, not being born in the United States, and all the information circulating around his birth certificate was a Feeding frenzy of gaslighting.

The email issues surrounding presidential candidate Hillary Rodham Clinton had monumental amount of gaslighting on both sides.

Moving forward into present day politics, gaslighting has become so standard that is difficult to imagine a political process without it.

President Donald Trump's Twitter feed, and the continued, unrestricted support by several media outlets, which refuse to say anything but good about him, along with the attempt to paint anyone who says anything negative as being wrong, liars, or unpatriotic, is almost totally composed of gaslighting.

Gaslighting on a societal level

As with most things in life, gaslighting not only occurs between people, on a personal level, it also occurs between groups and is the factor in society as a whole.

When it occurs between adults, who are presumed to be independent, the intended manipulation is generally considered bad

When the same information is provided to young children, in an organized manner, in order to teach them about our culture, our cultural beliefs systems, and our way of life, it is considered positive.

In this context we call it socialization.

When gaslighting is used by the media and nationwide outlets come as well as companies for advertising purposes it moves into the realm of propaganda.

As with all things, when the manipulation is used to present or teach something which is in line with our cultural values, it is considered good.

When the manipulation is done by companies, in advertising come in an effort to change the way you, the consumer perceives something, it may be good, bad, or neutral.

When the manipulation is done on a political scale, each incident needs to be judged on its own merit.

Critical Thinking: A Final Analysis.

What follows is a description of the movie "DEATH OF A NATION" directed by D'Sousza and released in 2018. After reading it, we will subject it to an analysis using basic critical thinking skills.

The Review:

Not since 1860 have the Democrats so fanatically refused to accept the result of a free election. That year, their target was Lincoln. They smeared him. They went to war to defeat him. In the end, they assassinated him. Now the target of the Democrats is President Trump and his supporters. The Left calls them racists, white supremacists and fascists. These charges are used to justify driving Trump from office and discrediting the right "by any means necessary." But which is the party of the slave plantation? Which is the party that invented white supremacy? Which is the party that praised fascist dictators and shaped their genocidal policies and was in turn praised by them? Moreover, which is the party of racism today? Is fascism now institutionally embodied on the right or on the left? Through stunning historical recreations and a searching examination of fascism and white supremacy, Death of a Nation cuts through progressive big lies to expose hidden history and explosive truths. Lincoln united his party and saved America from the Democrats for the first time. Can Trump and we come together and save America for the second time?

Answering the BASIC Questions…

Question 1: Who said it?

- The name of the reviewer was not provided. We can assume some things about them. They are praising the movie, which has an unmistakable conservative tone.

Does it matter who told you this?

- Yes! Reviews should be objective, otherwise they are simply another form of advertising.

<u>Question 2: What did they say?</u>

Did they give facts or opinions?

- The entire review appears to consist of opinion and questions which lead to specific opinions.

Did they provide all the facts?

- No, there was no attempt to provide a balanced argument. Many of the opinions pulled information out of context.

Did they leave anything out?

- Yes, they did not include basic facts.

<u>Question 3: Where did they say it?</u>

- The review was posted on a public website with no attempt to make it private. There is no opportunity to provide any rebuttal.

Question 4: When did they say it?

Was it before, during or after an important event?

- It was at the start of the movie's release to the general public. It appears to be an attempt to draw in a specific crowd in order to sell an idea, and therefore sell movie tickets.

Is timing important?

- Yes, the timing has the possibility of influencing ticket sales. You should assume this is one of the reason behind the release of the review. If it were presented after the movie had run, the possibility of this manipulation would be less.

Question 5: Why did they say it?

Did they explain the reasoning behind their opinion?

- No, it was just a recital of opinions.

Were they trying to make someone look good or bad?

- All of the opinions appear to show only one side of the facts of a debate. At first glance it would appear they were attempting to disparage Non-Conservatives and promote Conservatives.

<u>Question 6: How did they say it?</u>

Were they happy or sad, angry or indifferent?

- There was no clear tone to the opinion.

Did they write it or say it?

- It is written.

Could you understand what was said?

- Yes, it was clear. It was presented in an emotional format.

Let's break down the major sentences:

Not since 1860 have the Democrats so fanatically refused to accept the result of a free election.

- This is a huge statement with multiple implications. How has anyone "fanatically refused" to accept the election. The transition of power went on without any upsets. A testimony to our Democracy.
- What do they mean by "free election?" Clearly a majority of people feel Russia interfered with the election on some level.

- In fact all U.S. Intelligence Agencies believe Russia and Putin interfered. The question is how much and what was the effect.

- Certainly until those questions are answered it is not possible to call the election FREE.

That year, their target was Lincoln. They smeared him. They went to war to defeat him. In the end, they assassinated him.

- Clearly this sentence is designed to make you believe the Democrats plotted to kill President Lincoln. This is a theory I have never heard and would be laughable in most academic venues.

Democrats did not go to war to defeat Lincoln. The Confederacy did.

Now the target of the Democrats is President Trump and his supporters.

- This may be true. In this polarized party system, most people of one party target the head of the other party.
- It has no value in this review other than to suggest Democrats are operating on pure, unthinking hatred. It also assumes President Trump is unblemished.

The Left calls them racists, white supremacists and fascists. These charges are used to justify driving Trump from office and discrediting the right "by any means necessary."

- In this sentence, the focus should be on the first use of the word "them".

- Who is them?

- What do "them" believe?

- How does the common man drive a President from Office?

- There are ways to remove a President and they are enshrined in the Constitution.
- This is a use of the gaslighting strategy PLAYING THE VICTIM CARD.

But which is the party of the slave plantation?

- I don't know. Which one? This statement indicates that Democrats were pro-slavery and Republicans were not.

Which is the party that invented white supremacy?

- No party invented white supremacy. White supremacy is a belief system based on a racist and racial worldview.

Which is the party that praised fascist dictators and shaped their genocidal policies and was in turn praised by them?

- This sentence is so far out of reality it needs to be understood as simply a hyperbolic attempt to smear the other side. It is difficult to argue against a concept that is not grounded in reality.

Moreover, which is the party of racism today?

- Objectively, President Trump is the head of the Republican Party and has made multiple statements regarding the White Supremacists who protested in Charlottesville in 2018. He recognized them as "Good People".

Is fascism now institutionally embodied on the right or on the left?

- Fascism is defined as is a form of radical authoritarian ultra-nationalism, characterized by dictatorial power, forcible suppression of opposition and control of industry and commerce.
- Does either party, as a whole support this type of government?
- If they do, it is not apparent.

Through stunning historical recreations and a searching examination of fascism and white supremacy, Death of a Nation cuts through progressive big lies to expose hidden history and explosive truths.

- "Cuts through progressive big lies to expose hidden history and explosive truths."
- This is clearly an attack on one side by the other, without a basis in fact and not supported by any objective evidence. The only purpose to put this in the review is to characterize all non-conservatives as liars, who are hiding the TRUTH (Whatever that may be) to hide HISTORY (No specific historical event is noted, and finalizing with the statement that this HIDDEN HISTORY, upon being revealed will severely damage the non-conservative party.
- This is PROPAGANDA at its finest.

Lincoln united his party and saved America from the Democrats for the first time.

- I don't believe any historian would agree that Lincoln united his party, and certainly not from the Democrats. This sentence infers that the Democrats are an enemy invader attempting to destroy America.

Can Trump and we come together and save America for the second time?

- This infers that America is at a breaking point and needs to be saved. At this point in the review, the review has become so one-sided and propagandized, it collapses in upon itself.

Why did we take so much time with this review?

Because the cure for gaslighting is self-awareness and critical thinking. I hope this exercise in critical thinking helps you in your future relationships.

Gaslighting: a Summary:

Gaslighting is a psychological technique composed of several specific actions designed to manipulate individuals and situations and deny or obscure the truth.

Gaslighting is a form of psychological abuse and can be as damaging to the victim as physical and sexual abuse.

Like all psychological abuse, it is difficult to understand and identify.

Gaslighting in damaging, dangerous and just plain mean.

If you recognize yourself in any part of this book, find a therapist and get help.

Epilogue

How this book came to be.

I wanted to describe Gaslighting in a manner that everyone could understand, regardless of educational level of training. It is a slippery subject. I decided to write it in the form of a question and answer session as if I was asked by someone to explain it and we were sitting over a cup of coffee.

I decided to write the entire first draft in 10 days and then do one re-write for grammar and check all spelling. As I write this epilogue, it is Day 11.

Exhausting, scary and fun.

I hope you enjoy reading it as much as I enjoyed writing it.

About the Author

Harvey Norris is a Clinical Social Worker who has been practicing and training for 28 years. His specialties are in suicide prevention, aggression control training and post-traumatic stress. He currently works with Veterans and National Guardsmen in Central Louisiana.

He received his Master's in Social Work from Florida State University in 1990 and completed his clinical licensure in 1994. He has worked in child abuse investigations, with violent adolescents, foster care, juvenile probation, suicide prevention in state prison and county jail. He was a Suicide Prevention Coordinator for the Department of Veteran Affairs.

He currently provides training in "Crisis Intervention Techniques (CIT)" for the Alexandria Police Department, the St. Martin Parish Sheriff's Office and the Lafayette Parish Sheriff's Department. He is also a Deputy Sheriff St. Martin Parish.

His private practice is forensic and includes expert witness testimony for Wrongful Death by Suicide, Correctional Officer and Police Officer misconduct. He has provided deposition and courtroom testimony for District, Circuit, State and Federal Court. He has been admitted as an Expert Witness at all court levels.

He is the author or more than 10 books on clinical social work and his first non-fiction novel, <u>Murder by Cop</u> was published in May 2018.

APPENDIX

The Basic Method

<u>Question 1: Who said it?</u>
- Someone you know?
- Someone in a position of authority or power?
- Does it matter who told you this?

<u>Question 2: What did they say?</u>
- Did they give facts or opinions?
- Did they provide all the facts?
- Did they leave anything out?

<u>Question 3: Where did they say it?</u>
- Was it in public or in private?
- Did other people have a chance to respond and provide an alternative account?

<u>Question 4: When did they say it?</u>
- Was it before, during or after an important event?
- Is timing important?

Question 5: Why did they say it?
- Did they explain the reasoning behind their opinion?
- Were they trying to make someone look good or bad?

- Question 6: How did they say it?
  - Were they happy or sad, angry or indifferent?
  - Did they write it or say it?
  - Could you understand what was said?

The Critical Consensus Method

Activity 1: Analyzing
Separating or breaking a whole into parts to discover their nature, functional and relationships.
"I studied it piece by piece"
"I sorted things out

Activity 2: Applying Standards
Judging according to established personal, professional, or social rules or criteria.
"I judged it according to..."

Activity 3: Discriminating
Recognizing differences and similarities among things or situations and distinguishing carefully as to category or rank.
"I rank ordered the various..."
"I grouped things together"

Activity 4: Information Seeking
Searching for evidence, facts, or knowledge by identifying relevant sources and gathering objective, subjective, historical, and current data from those sources.

"I knew I needed to lookup/study..."
"I kept searching for data."

Activity 5: Logical Reasoning
Drawing inferences or conclusions that are supported in or justified by evidence.
"I deduced from the information that..."
"My rationale for the conclusion was..."
Activity 6: Predicting
Envisioning a plan and its consequences.
"I envisioned the outcome would be..."
"I was prepared for..."
Activity 7: Transforming Knowledge
Changing or converting the condition, nature, form, or function of concepts among contexts.
"I improved on the basics by..."
"I wondered if that would fit the situation of ..."

Courtesy of B. K. Scheffer and M.G. Rubenfeld, "A Consensus Statement on Critical Thinking in Nursing," Journal of Nursing Education, 39, 352-9 (2000).